A Pocket Siz
for Parent
and
The Aut'  n

Paul Isaacs

Foreword by Prof. Tony Attwood

chipmunkapublishing
the mental health publisher

Published by

Chipmunkapublishing

http://www.chipmunkapublishing.com

Copyright © Paul Isaacs 2013

ISBN   978-1-84991-970-8

Chipmunkapublishing   gratefully   acknowledge   the support of Arts Council England.

Index

Introduction by Author

Paul Isaacs Author of "Living Through The Haze" © Isaacs Family

The Autistic Spectrum

Introduction

Hello there readers! My name is Paul Isaacs. I was born on the 7th May 1986. My parents are Belinda and Peter Isaacs, and from an early age they (in particular my Mum) knew there were "differences" in my initial development and as I got older the more apparent these "differences" became.

I was diagnosed at the age of 24 in 2010 with High Functioning Autism and later diagnosis of this is commonplace for many people on the autism spectrum. I am no exception in that respect. However, my development in my early infancy was that of a child with *"Classic"* and/or *"Kanner's Autism"* that means by today's recognition of the spectrum and person with an ASD (*Autistic Spectrum Disorder*) and an SLD (*Severe Learning Disability*) or the Autism is so severe that the person is finding communicating very difficult and so for many years that would be the case for me in terms of development and cognitive skills.

Foreword by Professor Tony Attwood

I first met Paul at a conference for parents and professionals in Oxford. He had a session within the program to explain his personal experience of having autism and offer his practical advice for the audience. During his presentation I was spellbound, as was the audience of several hundred people. We were amazed at his charismatic eloquence, insight and sense of humour and he received thunderous applause from a very appreciative audience. Now his insights and wisdom are available for a wider audience in the form of a pocket sized guide. This is a small book, but there is valuable advice on every page, and as it is so small, the clear explanations and practical strategies are quick to read and absorb.

Paul uses as examples his own experiences as he matured from a child with classic autism to an employed and independent adult. He is able to explain to the reader why he behaved in ways that can be confusing for family members, peers and teachers. The content is consistent with the diagnostic criteria for Autism Spectrum Disorders and the theoretical models developed by psychologists, but the engaging and endearing qualities of the book are his descriptions in plain language of being autistic, and his ability to offer sage advice that will benefit parents, professionals and especially children and adults who have autism.

Tony Attwood

December 2012

Experiences as a Child with Classic Autism

Me at 6 Months of Age in October 1986 - notice the left eye is turning inwards and my right eye is "distant" this is a sign of visual fragmentation issues © Isaacs Family

When I was a little boy I lived in a very sensory based world with little to no functional language at all. My favourite interests were flushing toilets, primary colours (reds, greens, blues etc.), TV tunes such as *"Blind Date"* and *"Blockbusters"* and so forth. I didn't really engage with children that much, if at all, and because of this the world was like a massive puzzle to me with lots of smells, shapes and colours, so people were not my priority at all! I was half aware they existed but I got caught up in my interests so quickly that I would forget where I was, whom I was with and sometimes even myself. I was so hooked on the small moments that the bigger stuff wasn't even processing (I wasn't even aware that it was "there" to process). This sort of behaviour went on for many years and it wasn't until later in my infancy that functional speech came at around 7 or 8 years old. This meant that I was in Year 4 at primary school at the time.

Autism & School

I learnt the hard way I suppose on how to socialise and school is a massive hive of social activity from talking about relationships, friendships which were forming, breaking up and reforming around me. Small talk, for example, *"so what is the next door neighbour doing renovating his or her house."* I still have problems with small talk because it doesn't have a journey, so when I did pick up the rythm of the conversation with all phonics intact I still didn't understand the purpose or the meaning of the topic of conversation.

These things just didn't appeal to me. I wanted to talk about my topic and I would try and listen to the teacher or the student and this wouldn't work because of my language processing skills.

Managing processing was a massive issue at school for me. I had problems with lights, colours, reflections, face blindness, body disconnections (brain and "body awareness signals"), body language blindness, visual fragmentation (object & meaning blindness), receptive and expressive language problems.

Things to know

1. *Eye contact can be difficult. Try and focus on an area which isn't as "uncomfortable" to focus such as the nose, mouth or the brow.*
2. *Engage in other topics with students or if that is too uncomfortable find students and teachers that share a similar interest to build self–esteem.*
3. *Teachers and students must understand that if an autistic is stimming (rocking, hand flapping etc.) that could be the student's way of showing signs of happiness or discomfort and it is up to*

the teacher to find out triggers for certain types of behaviour to help the autistic. Stimming should NEVER be stopped.

4. *Sensory issues must be taken into account. This will affect learning, mental health and wellbeing of the person with ASD, they affect learning and processing of information causing pain, discomfort and meltdowns. The teacher must be made aware of these issues and implement help for the student such as time out from lessons, one to one tutoring (in sensory "safe" environment).*

5. *Information processing may vary from day to day. The teacher must be made aware of the processing fluctuation in the student with ASD and the exploration of communication must always be person centred.*

Social Skills or Academic Achievement?

Well, it's interesting which comes first. I would say in order for the person with ASD to truly harness his or her skills is to build up their social awareness such as learning how to share toys, which I slowly developed by my Mother making me go out to play with other children in the neighbourhood. Acquiring the *meaning* of the words "*Please*" and "*Thank you*" and processing and understanding the basics and the beauty of human kindness. However, there are many ways a person with ASD can show you their thanks without using words but through simple gestures that are on a spiritual level that sometimes people don't understand. Social skills is a broad, sometimes generic term, but people with ASD use social skills in a *different* way to typical people. It is less about conformity and more about embracing what the person with ASD can do. Not trying to make them be something which they're not.

One of the most important things I've learnt is to say the word "*Sorry*". But what must also be taken into account is that the foundation and reason for saying sorry must be just, and the clear foundation of understanding must be there. I have seen many students with ASD being *forced* to say sorry for behaviours that others have deemed unacceptable. This is unfair. The true meaning of the word sorry must be instilled on a moral basis and not as a means of controlling the autistic person. If there is no foundation for the meaning the act of saying sorry will be lost.

The true skill to apologise will benefit the child and teenager into his and her adulthood which will help to not only mend broken relationships and friendships but also make interacting and criticism less of an issue.

I suppose I should elaborate further on why social skills should come first. It is quite simple, if the child with ASD has a budding interest in biology or mathematics and gets straight As and goes into further education such as college and university. If he or she hasn't learnt any social understanding, how will they cope in a working environment in which their interest is their job? The academic achievements could become void and this could in turn develop into a worrying trade off. This can sadly lead into incidents of bullying, neglect and exploitation on the part of the autistic individual because of peers misunderstanding the *"core"* issues behind the behaviours.

You've harnessed the academic skills but not the social skills and it leaves the person with ASD penalised because of this. I think *person centred* social skills should always come first with individuals with ASD. That comes with respecting the person with ASD and their way of communicating and interacting. Skills that they need for life should be a positive balance between the *social* and *academic* (but remember it's the person's choice what they would like to do in life). This creates a positive and realistic outcome for the child. But remember that the person with autism, including myself, will have their own unique perspective of what *"social"* is and their own unique take on it. Also remember there are many different ways of communicating other than speech, this is a way which I learned but always remember to be *person centred* with the person with ASD, and understand how they want to be social and how they communicate, that is the key.

Things to know

> 1. *Harness their social skills (manners and social etiquette within the realms of the autistic person's understanding and needs without hidden agendas such as control, bullying and exploitation).*
>
> 2. *Harness their interests (people with autism have a passion for many things; if it has a positive effect on their life thrive in it and encourage it).*
>
> 3. *Remember that what is behind ASD is a person and these skills are good but it's the way in which you teach them; being with "one's selfhood" is a fine balance between teaching and learning a skill but not losing a part of the person due to conformity (it's ok to be autistic!).*

> 4. *Remember to respect the ASD way of socialising and how they have their unique take on it.*

Male Competitiveness and Androgyny

This is something an HFA boy will come to recognise soon enough. The social rules of being a "boy", gender traits and even gender blurring can occur as typically people with HFA do not recognise stereotypes (for example blue is for a boy and pink for a girl). I could go on to say that I found the company of girls much more interesting than boys because they talked differently. The overall aspect was that girls would be more accepting of my *social faux pas*. I certainly do not consider myself as overly masculine and I think androgynous would be accurate.

Some females on the spectrum are considered to be "tomboys". I think the same can be applied to males on the spectrum in the sense that they can be feminine. It is like Prof Baron-Cohen *"Extreme Male Brain"* Theory but turned on its head.

Male competitive conversations I will have to say is still a hard one to grasp for me. These sorts of conversations are very hard to understand, illogical and pointless from my perspective. The interesting aspect that the person with HFA could actually gain from these competitive conversations is some "middle-ground", which in many scenarios would be beneficial such as in a team meeting the person with HFA could just state a seemingly random idea to the panel contributing to the discussion and bringing into focus. This is also a valid example of teamwork and a *why* for the person with HFA to get through these sorts of conversations.

Alcohol

Peer pressure is something we all go through and if it's not a tempting sip of Uncle Bert's whiskey from the drinks cabinet to the smoking of cigarettes it'll be something else. I would like to say that one of the positive aspects of autism is not all are succumbing to these stereotypical (or neurotypical) peer pressures such as clothes or the type of rucksack you "*need*" to have. Some of these teenage peer pressures are dangerous and appealing. One of them is alcohol; it's a dangerous substance if abused and it causes countless problems in later life such as mental health problems like depression to serious organ abuse such as liver and kidney failure.

Having an ASD can create feelings of guilt and unease of being one's self and methinks unfortunately the aspect of drinking can become very tempting to people on the spectrum. It could be considered a rite of passage onto the neurotypical world. It can also be sadly enough an escape from everyday struggles of life and what may be most appealing is the "change" of personality; the person with HFA may *feel* more "socially able" after drinking. This can unfortunately lead down the dark path to alcohol dependence and people with HFA having trouble with criticism and a very large capacity to have arguments. I didn't see alcohol as an outlet for my problems during my teenage years luckily but it can happen and preventative measures should be taken.

Things to Know

1. *Check what type of "friends" your son or daughter is spending time with.*
2. *Promote that alcohol dependence is a BAD thing and will cause social regression, isolation and alcohol related diseases.*

> 3. *Improve the awareness of the damage this could do to your son or daughter's mental and physical health.*
>
> 4. *Try getting to the "core" of the problems and create a person centred pathway for autistic individual.*

Social Aspects of the Workplace

The workplace is a massive glob of social domination. How does someone with autism possibly exist with other co-workers? May be going in with a spacesuit and saying *"Hi, I'm from planet Autie, I come in peace!"*

Well, it is all to do with judgement and experience, and the benefit is I can look at a lot of my mistakes in retrospect and make sure whoever is reading this does not make the same mistakes. The first thing is the staff room which can be one big problem for someone with ASD because gossip is always prominent and arguments could also be on the agenda. It used to amaze me how tired I used to get after spending an hour's lunch break up in a staff room. My work output decreased and I could have quite easily gone home. The noises, language, sight and sounds were all too much for me to process. So how can people with ASD get around this tricky scenario?

Things to know 1

> 1. *Go out during breaks, it calms you down and you can build your resources back up for when you return to work*
> 2. *Take a magazine/paper/article anything of interest which will pass the time*
> 3. *Don't feel you have to justify going out if a member of staff enquires why you do so*

The issue is judging who you can speak to and defining a work colleague or acquaintance from a friend at work. This is very hard to do because of having an ASD one of the main issues is that it's a grey area, and in my case it was a trial and error period. I must say I was bullied at work because of this and also because I was socially naive and entrusted people with a lot of personal information about myself. I also had the common route of declaring my special interest to work colleagues. I had the naive assumption that when people "grew up" they weren't childish anymore and didn't bully; how wrong I was. In fact, I would say that adults can be *much* worse and cause long term damage to your confidence and mental health. Bullies do grow up and they find jobs just like the rest of us. Here are some tips to help you evade these issues.

Things to know 2

1. *Befriend someone who is genuine or try and find someone who has the same interest as you (you never know they may have an ASD also).*
2. *Do not give out personal information.*
3. *Ask your parents for opinions of people's actions or behaviour within the workplace that you are confused about or feel threatened by.*
4. *Find a placement in work where your concentration is not diverted and is free from distractions of work colleagues.*
5. *Ask your parents to try defining "colleague/acquaintance" & "friend" to improve judgement skills.*

The Confusion & the Beauty of the workplace

© Isaacs 2012

Speaking About Thoughts and Feelings

For people with ASD this can be a challenging thing to do because it involves a great deal in gauging one's own feelings. It is important not to assume that someone else knows how you feel because that can cause an "out of the blue" scenario where you bottle up your feelings for so long it causes an eruption of emotions. This was what happened a lot at school for me. I was the joker, the happy cartoon funny guy (this was to do with dissociation), but inside I was hurting. This was prominent during my school years in particular. In my secondary school years the only way I could gain acceptance was *"The Joker"* personality which caused memory loss and a false perception of time, but after I came home from school it would be an explosion and unfortunately it was my parents that got the anger which should have been vented on the people at school and sometimes it did.

Things to know

> 1. *Talk to your parents about your feelings. You could use objects, pretend parallel situations (talking as if it is happening to someone else). Many people with ASDs have problems with theory of mind (mindblindness) and putting themselves into other people's situations.*
> 2. *Write your feelings down.*
> 3. *Discuss various outcomes to these situations (challenging concrete thinking).*
> 4. *Discuss intervention techniques for future outbursts and challenging behaviours. Find out the "triggers" and the mechanics behind them.*

> 5. *Alexithymia affects 85% of people with ASDs. It is an inability to process thoughts and emotions in a typical way.*

Public Transport

This can be a scary and sometimes a seemingly impossible task for someone with ASD to even use public transport. There could be an array of not only social but sensory and anxiety issues which could prevent this seemingly easy task of getting on the bus or train a real issue. Exposure anxiety which can be a problem from my personal experience is a state of consciousness where you don't want people to "see" a part of yourself or your identity causing you to withdraw.

A person on the spectrum may benefit from sitting in a particular place and position on the bus (window seat), mine is nearly always on the left on a double decker and on the right on a single decker. Confidence is the real issue here as the first person you meet is the bus driver. I have found social interaction with bus drivers a struggle over the years. Sometimes if I'm in a heightened state the noise of the people chattering on the bus can be overwhelming and weird and also people sitting next to me can be an issue. Here are some tips for public transport.

Things to know

1. *Prepare yourself in advance: what bus or train are you waiting for? Does it have a number? What time will it arrive at the station?*
2. *Have a mentor, friend or support worker come with you.*
3. *Have your money or ticket prepared before you get onto the bus.*
4. *Have a mental check of what you are about to say to the bus driver. Remember to be clear and direct.*
5. *Listen to the driver when he or she asks for a fare.*
6. *Sensory issues such as <u>language processing problems, auditory agnosias and visual agnosias may be an issue.</u>*
7. *Take ear muffs, headphones, earplugs for noise.*

> 8. *Take sunglasses, tinted lenses for visual fragmentation.*
>
> 9. *Take an item of interest and/or comfort to help calm you.*

Shops

Now, shopping in public areas involves lots of noise and crowds of people, but you want that favourite *Dr Who DVD* which you have been waiting a whole month for. People with ASD have special interests which will no doubt bring them into contact with shops and shopping centres. This can bring about bouts of panic attacks and social confusion in shops because of sensory overload such as noise, lights, images, reflections, surfaces and also communication and language issues with the members of staff.

Things to know

> 1. *Keep focused on what you're looking for, remember which section of the shop it is in (such as a video game, DVD or another item of interest).*

2. *Look for places in the shop which are quiet, this could give you time to prepare yourself to look in the shop.*

3. *Remember to bring enough money and check how much the product is.*

4. *When you have purchased your item make a mental note of the satisfaction you get from doing this, it builds confidence and self esteem.*

5. *If the shop and/or building is too much then leave!*

6. *Social interaction can be draining so remember to have food and water and items of comfort so you can reduce the risk of meltdown and anxiety.*

7. *Remember to have a mentor, support worker or friend with you.*

Restaurants

These situations can be tough and it's a big thing for a person with ASD to go into a restaurant. It deals with some of the issues that were stated in the shopping section such as sensory overload and social confusion. It's also down to "*on the spot*" (a very quick) decision making. What food would you like? What drink would you like?

Confidence skills are also required for you to give the right answers to the right questions. Another thing can be "audio distortion" where noise becomes this massive blob of unstructured sounds. I remember being in a pub restaurant with my Mum in one of our favourite pub restaurants, she was talking to me and a lady in front of us had a rather loud voice. I was looking at my Mum, her mouth was moving but I couldn't decipher what was coming out because the lady's voice had become dominant.

Things to know

1. *Choose a quiet spot in the restaurant; make sure you're not in anyone's eye line (remember eye contact can be an issue with someone you know let alone someone you don't!)*
2. *Think about what you would like to have and try to memorise it or keep hold of the menu until the waiter or waitress comes.*
3. *If you have a regular meal at this place to reduce anxiety you may like to choose that meal again (this has helped me over the years!)*

4. *Remember to (and if not try to) enjoy yourself. That is what going to a restaurant is all about. If it is too much in terms of communication and sensory issues there is no shame in leaving.*

5. *Always bring an item of interest and comfort (for anxiety and to calm down).*

Autism Friendly Social Groups

These groups can be a great asset to people with ASDs. They can be a place to go and escape or a place to extend their social network and so on. I have continued to go to such a group for over two years now and I have got a lot out of being there because I can relate to the people in a positive aspect. Many times you hear and read about the problems people with ASD have but let's try and be assertive and think of the benefits of being on the spectrum. Being in such a group surely challenges the perception of what ASD really is. Is it the fact that we could have twenty individuals in a room who happen to have ASD and they're all socialising, is that so hard to imagine?

Certainly not! It gives me and others such a confidence boost when I go there I can talk about my interests and they likewise can talk about their own topics of interest too.

These places are needed and I would like to see in the future at least one in every town and city in the UK. What can they give to a person with ASD?

Things to know

---

1. *This is a perfect place for someone who may have low self-esteem; it's a brilliant tool to gain confidence.*
2. *Sharing your special interests.*
3. *Expanding your social network and improving social skills.*
4. *A form of relaxation and "down time".*
5. *It's a positive place to be and that is what should be promoted throughout the group.*
6. *You can go there when you like.*

Autism & Friendships

This can be a very hard aspect to having an ASD as it's not just the creating of such a person but is maintaining that friendship that can be the issue. Believe me I'm talking from experience when friendships just seem to come and go out of nowhere or the person seems too angry or upset with me for no particular reason. I, however, don't have much of a drive for lots of friends, I'm happy with the one's I have made. I am also not interested in having a sexual or romantic relationship with someone. I like my autonomy; I live in a sensory based world and relate a lot to objects and things. I consider them my friends because they never harm, judge or hurt me. They are a source of comfort to me and have been since I was a young boy.

There are many people with ASDs who strongly want a social network and this can hurt the most when the person feels *so* sure that this friendship is going to work. From my experience the friends I have with ASDs seem to have a secret bond that not many people would begin to understand, it's like we know what each other's got and we may be saying secretly to each other "*yes* I understand you more just as you understand me more than someone else". It's like the Lord of the Flies but much nicer as there is a pact with one another.

One of the most redeeming traits my parents say I have is my sense of loyalty and the totality that comes with that. I try and help others in times of need and reassure them that things will be fine. I enjoy helping others; it makes me feel like a better person, because I genuinely care. I know that people with ASDs have this beautiful and entrusting trait which should be nurtured and *NEVER* exploited. I think that people with ASDs despite the difficulties can be good friends. Let's focus on the positives of what people with ASDs can bring to a friendship.

Things to know

1. *Loyalty*
2. *Kindness and consideration*
3. *Defend you (with strong senses of morality)*
4. *With the right chemistry can be "a friend for life"*
5. *Give out advice in a strong logical way*
6. *Good at one to one conversations*
7. *Can help you in times of need*

Autism Bases

This is an area I feel very strongly about because this can dictate a lot of what will happen in your child's life. Autism bases are an integral part of the child and parents' lives. It is a place where they learn all the skills that neurotypical people take for granted. I feel that more money should be spent on these places and that they should be expanded further and are more in the forefront of the national consciousness; that would be a big help. Although I never went to a base as I child I have been currently attending one as a volunteer. This has helped me realise the effort and dedication that comes through from the teachers and support workers that do this tremendous job of looking after and teaching these children who are on all different areas of the autistic spectrum.

How can this help your child?

1. *Autistic specific support which I can't emphasise enough how important it is for your child to get this; it is paramount for life skills in the future.*
2. *It's recognition of the child's ASD; this can help in further education and so on (that is of course a person centred choice for the child in the future).*
3. *This will benefit the child's social skills and social awareness.*
4. *This will benefit the child's life skills.*

> 5. *The knowledge within the base means other co-morbid conditions can be recognised (such as ADHD, Dyspraxia, Dyscalculia, Agnosias) and other learning difficulties, processing disorders, auto-immune disorders (gluten free food for example).*

Late Diagnosis

When I was eventually diagnosed with HFA in late 2010 it wasn't a shock at all. I had known from sixteen years old that something was *"different"* about me but it never had a name, it was just something I knew. I did some research when I was eighteen but nothing came of it because my parents confirmed to me at that time that there was nothing wrong. I can understand why they did this; it must have been a very scary thought for them to know that their son had a form of autism. I had been building up research to the point where I knew I had HFA, but to be told is a completely different set of circumstances because it is confirmation of what you have got not just logical speculation.

I went through many complications during that time and an inaccurate diagnosis by a Mental Health Specialist in

2008 prior to this didn't help me or my family. After I was told I had at that time *"Asperger traits with a complex personality"* I was discharged with no help or guidance, just a few pages of links to ASD social groups and that was it. This is where I think the whole system of diagnosis should be changed because you should get support afterwards, it is vital for your mental health.

Statistics show that people with ASDs are more likely to get depression throughout their lifetime and I am no exception. After finally getting the recognition of HFA in 2010 I didn't go into *"Denial Mode"*. It can be a very confusing and dangerous time for people who have been diagnosed later in life; it can produce a lot of negativity about the past and how it could have been a lot different. I'm pleased to say I have overcome this with the help of my family and friends. You have to realise that a diagnosis is a positive thing.

Things to know

> 1. *It's recognition of who you are but at the same time you are an individual.*
> 2. *This will help you, family and friends.*

> 3. *You have always had an ASD, you were born with this condition, it hasn't "just appeared".*
>
> 4. *Keep positive and find support from friends and family if you feel unhappy or depressed.*
>
> 5. *Get in contact with local charities or the NAS which will give help and advice on how to cope.*
>
> 6. *Go to ASD friendly social groups this can help you feel more happy with yourself.*

I would like to say that this is a positive aspect of your life not a negative one. It's a choice to perceive it like this. People with ASDs aspire to do a lot of good things which are personal to them.

Helping Others on the Spectrum

This had been a really positive experience and one that I think can benefit other people. As I stated earlier I have been doing volunteer work at an autism base and it has helped me a lot in understanding myself and relating to the children also. Like having friends on the spectrum the same thing applies here; you have a secret bond of understanding that others may not have. It has been a privilege to be a part of the work team and to assist with the children. This may be a future endeavour (for anybody reading this) you may like to pursue and I personally think that people with ASDS working in autism bases will be a huge asset to the team.

Things to know

---

1. *You understand the child may be from more of an emotional aspect and have an inside out approach to their behaviours which you can discuss with the fellow co-workers too.*

2. *The teachers understand the child from an academic perspective and gain a different type of social understanding and approach which the person on the spectrum can understand.*

3. *As a result everyone (yourself, students and staff) is benefiting from your ASD experience.*

Criticism

It's a hard thing to be criticised and *even* more so for people with HFA. I can remember many times when I would go on the defensive and argue and argue my point as the valid one. This is due to mindblindness and the complications of seeing others' points of view.

Concrete thinking also plays a part in this issue, as well as thinking in a very "black" & "white" way. In a job situation if a person was to be criticised and the individual with an ASD was to react in a very violent way this would cause problems with work relations and potentially the job itself. How can this problem with criticism be avoided?

Things to know

---

1. *In this case the person dealing out the criticism would need knowledge of ASD and how to talk in a clear and structured manner.*
2. *Try and understand that the person may be trying to help you, not attack you.*
3. *Try not to go on the defensive.*

> 4. *Ask the person in question to write their points down.*
>
> 5. *If there is still a misunderstanding the person with ASD may need the information repeated.*

Be Happy With Yourself

That is one of the crucial things that everybody has the right to be happy with their own self, which can be an issue with people who have ASD. You need to find a place in which you feel wanted but in order to get there you must already be balanced, is that you can't rely on other people to make you happy, you must be happy.

Think about where you are and how positive that is. You may find this through your talents of art or computing or the fact that you have cleaned up your bedroom and vacuum cleaned the downstairs sitting room. They can be big things, they can be little things, but they still count. Everything counts in the long run as anything positive builds the road to happiness, and if people you like want to come along let them join. Positive people equal a healthy clear mind; this will reduce all the anxieties and meltdowns that occur when you have ASD or lessen them to a degree which is more manageable. Here are a few tips to a healthy mind.

Things to know

1. *Try and think in the now because in theory you are always there.*
2. *Choose positive people such as friends and family to be around you.*
3. *Look at your strengths.*

Mum & Gramp "Sensing the Calm" after Autism Oxford Event

© Isaacs/Harpwood 2012

Relationships

The unique thing that is occurring in ASD is that one can have a relationship, and why not, it is a human feeling to love and want another. Some people with an ASD will stay single for the rest of their lives, like myself, others will pursue a partner. I must admit I don't have a partner but I think I can still give some knowledge on the subject from an outsider looking in.

Things to know

1. *You may want to find a person with similar interests or who has ASD themselves.*

2. *There may be clubs or dating agencies that specifically cater for people with ASD around the area.*

3. *Think about what you would like to say to them and where you would like to meet up.*

4. *Ask people for advice on this subject such as your parents or older siblings who would guide you on this subject.*

Mum & Dad whom are both on the spectrum in their early 20s

Grandparents 50th Anniversary My Grandfather has Asperger's Syndrome

© Isaacs/Harpwood 2012

Starting Your Own ASD Group

As I have stated earlier the positive aspects of joining and being part of an ASD Group is that you could start one yourself. This could be an excellent outlet for people within your area to come and join and share in the enjoyment of being part of a group. The person with HFA could make new friends and expand his or her social network. It also could bring about a new dynamic and create community interest which could benefit everybody in the group including their parents and relatives. You have to take into account the environment, so here are a few elements to take into account when you are thinking of creating a group.

Things to know

1. *Space, and make sure there is lots of it, maybe a room with neutral colours which aren't too "hard" on the eye.*
2. *Make sure the light is soft and not too overpowering in the room.*
3. *The position of the chairs may be a factor also, depending on the individuals that come.*

> 4. That you have a room which is secluded and doesn't have a lot of background noise.
>
> 5. Over all make sure the individuals have fun. That's what the group is all about. Make sure you find a place which doesn't have a reputation for trouble and that the people in the establishment are accepting of people with ASDs and the unusual behaviour that comes with it.

Does Autism Run In The Family?

You have friends with an ASD so why couldn't a family member (and a whole lot of other family members) have it? The chances are very high indeed. Hans Asperger himself recognised that the father and son were very similar in behaviours. This is certainly true with my Father in particular, although his difficulties were recognised early on in his life when he was put into a special education school from the ages of five until eleven; his social skills were rigid and his obsessions were intense. At this point there was no name for what condition he had, it was in the late sixties until early seventies that he was at the special education school. Today he still has obsessions that still exist, from weight training to learning Tai Chi. He doesn't like functions or social events very much but tries his best to fit in, which he has learned from experience. He was diagnosed with Asperger's Syndrome in 2010. My Mother is also the same where she puts a "mask" on for social events and gatherings, which is a common thing for women with ASDs to do in social situations, and they both become very tired during these events because of the enormous amount of concentration that is put into socialising. She was diagnosed with Atypical Autism in 2010. Can it run further than your parents? The answer is yes, of course it can. My Grandfather has many obvious characteristics of Autism and was diagnosed in 2011. He has four main subject areas which are as follows:

1. *Football (Oxford United)*

2. *Weather*

3. *Gardening*

4. *Politics*

Like me, through talking to him about his experiences, he has Social Emotional Agnosia. To simplify it means he has *body language blindness* and doesn't *read* the subtle signs of emotion that are perceived through looking at a person's face or body language. His records of some of his intense interests can be found in the book cabinet in his home. It's what I call his *"logic"* diary which ironically doesn't have a word or sentence about his own emotions but has weather readings such as the amount of rainfall or how hot it was in a day. I feel that my parents and my Grandfather have all done very well indeed. This may help others that are in need of some personal exploration that there are others in the family with ASD. Here is how you can go about it.

Things to ask

---

1. *Ask questions that are ASD related to your parents or family members.*
2. *You could in turn ask them about their Parents and Grandparents.*
3. *Piece together any particular behaviours that seem unusual or eccentric.*
4. *You could figuratively build a family tree and see how far ASDs in your family goes back.*
5. *I know of at least another four members of my family that potentially have an ASD and it certainly explains why I am the way I am.*

My Dad & I (as a severely autistic infant) when I was 3 years old

The Concept of "Loner"

This word is used in a negative way to describe a person who likes his or her own company. In fact it's a word used in the diagnostic criteria. It can also be used to offend or belittle somebody's personality. I think that the term "loner" should at least be put into the proper context; there is nothing wrong with liking one's own company, not at all. People with ASD do like their own company. I can give a perfect example of how this can help strip the negative implications of being branded in such a way. When I was at primary school and I was in the classroom that was a time for listening to your teacher and (trying) to learn, then lunchtime would come and I would go outside. My downtime was to be on my own, it was a way of preparing myself for the next lesson to come, be it Maths or English or whatever it was, a way of relaxing and being at one with myself. I used it subconsciously as a tool for coping and managing my academic output and learning potential without consciously realising this at the time. Here are the benefits of being a loner.

Things to know

---

1. *You set your own agenda, you don't rely on others.*
2. *In many ways your form of free time is not dictated by others.*
3. *You can relax and create stress relief.*
4. *You are happy with this.*

Parents should not always worry that their autistic child is alone because ironically they may be happy to be so and that can continue into teenage and adult years. They may build friendships in their late teens and early twenties, it's never too late. But don't think of being a loner or your child being alone as a bad thing because at that point in time it may be their preference.

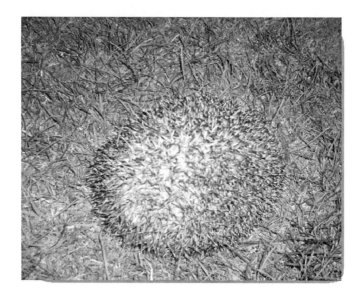

Hedgehog In our garden symbolising the "loner" who is happy to be left alone

© Isaacs 2012

Special Interests

I have mentioned these a lot through the certain examples. For years the child with ASD, like me, will flip through many obsessions with information about one particular subject. I can remember the sheer joy of getting a big book on the *"Titanic"* and reading about the measurements of the ship, its funnels, cargo and the amount of people on board. I also liked reading about the *"White Star Line"* the company that owned the vessel. It's these sorts of interests that bring back fond memories of enjoyment and excitement for me as a child. Now I'm an adult I'm still going to have special interests which I like to talk and research about. It's part of having ASD and I think it's a good part, don't you think?

Other than that I still have interests in colours, textures, movement, light and things that spin and make noises. A lot of "sensory" interests bear no language because it is not needed. Those base sensory interests have stayed with me well into adulthood and continue to be with me. I consider them a blessing in times of crisis and friends in times of need. So in terms of a special interest it can be something that brings joy to a person that is purely on a sensory based level, not always an information based level.

The ability to take in knowledge of a particular interest will be much quicker. Some people with ASD may have a savant-like memory for all the facts and details of a particular subject. This to me is the creation not only of a vast amount of knowledge for the person with ASD, but also a vast amount of happiness. Ask anybody with ASD and there is nothing (well almost) more they would like to do than engage in their interest. This is because people with ASD have a different way of processing information and this is one of the assets, taking in knowledge and what becomes of that, not power but happiness. I can honestly say that I'm very happy looking through my interests. Here are the benefits.

1. *It's time well spent.*
2. *It's relaxing for the person with ASD.*
3. *It can sometimes create career prospects.*
4. *It creates happiness and positivistic results like I have mentioned about the HFA friendly groups; it's always nice to find someone who shares your special interest and likewise for that person as well.*

This light toy has so many meanings and reasons I love the colours, movement and shapes it makes me relax and feel calm

© Isaacs 2012

Organisation Skills

These things can be quite a trial in themselves. I would have to say that I have still a long way to go to master the true art of organisation but the concept of trying must be promoted and that we must never give up.

Some people with ASD have, like me, terrible organisation skills but I have learned that what is a big help is my yearly timetable. It has clear text and numbers with enough space to write in your activities for the day. It also has coloured stickers which I have embraced as each sticker has a purpose. Other things are sticking reminders and important phone numbers on my bedroom cabinet door. This helps with many different aspects of life and doesn't make one panic (like I have done many times) when I can't find a phone number.

People with ASDs *need* structure. It's a foundation point for everything and getting the concept early about organising is a brilliant thing, it will save a lot of upset in the future.

How to help

1. *Have a timetable or graph preferably a yearly planner.*
2. *Have different symbols for different events, e.g. red is for doctor's appointments and yellow is for meeting up with friends.*

> 3. *Ask for assistance if times and dates have to be changed. Enjoy the process of organising, it will help in the long run.*

Gaining Independence Skills

These are essential skills that people, even more so with ASDs, should learn. It will be the backbone of their lives. There are many ways of gaining these skills. The best way, I feel, is experiencing them and being practical with them. In order for someone with ASD to truly know what it's like to buy something from the supermarket is to do it with assistance from a parent and to go through the process slowly. As I have got older I still have to be prompted to do things. For example, my Mother teaching me how to mow the lawn on my own was a long but rewarding task. I have to admit I find difficultly in turning the mower and coordinating that movement feels very clumsy indeed but it's through commitment that the individual will get there. Everybody has the right to have an independent life. Here is what will help with that life within the parameters of their abilities.

1. *Financial Skills such as budgeting and money management.*

2. *Learning how to wash and hang clothes out to dry.*

3. *Tidying up in the house and the garden.*

4. *Using and feeling comfortable with public transport.*

5. *Looking after the parent's house and gaining the sense of responsibility.*

The Keys of Life

Holidays

This can be a stressful time for someone with ASD. The aspect of going to an unfamiliar place can be quite terrifying indeed. My parents did take me on holidays; it was an interesting experience. I can safely say they have always been very supportive with me. Looking back there was an anxiety but I'm convinced it was lessened by my parents' way of just doing things when we were on holiday.

An ideal thing that my parents started to do as I got older was to not check into hotels where it can become very alien and scary but rent out a cottage say for a week. We all liked our own company, it was home from home, and we did the same things we would do at home. My Father would buy the shopping, my Mother would cook. When we went to bed we were in separate bedrooms. All those senses of familiarity were very important for me (and for all of us really) when we were on holiday. So here is how it can be done.

Tips for Holidays

1. *Instead of a hotel rent a cottage or small house.*
2. *Make sure it's a quiet place with limited noise e.g. villages.*
3. *Make the place feel like a home by bringing a book or something that is to do with your special interest.*
4. *This will be a great confidence builder and will help with a lot of self- esteem issues. It's very easy with ASD just to be stuck in your home or up in your bedroom but to make a holiday as enjoyable for the whole family is the main aim, and helping with transition from home to holiday destination will help.*

Autism & Finding One's Niche

When I had lost two jobs this negative feeling was very prominent in my head and when you think this false belief is right this only makes you go down deeper into despair. It is at this point that action needs to be taken and you could have all the support in the world but if you can't see that this negative strand needs to be broken - you will eventually have to. Having ASD can make you very sensitive to *having* an ASD and its odd form of self-reflection. I have learnt that I am my own person and that I have qualities that are just as valid as the next person's. It's to do with self-belief of what is reality and fiction.

1. *Don't compare in a negative context, it will make you feel low.*
2. *Don't make a lot of unfair self-judgments about yourself.*
3. *Don't make derogative comments about yourself e.g. retard, stupid.*
4. *Think about what makes you happy and the positive aspects of your life.*

Symbolism of Growth, Happiness and finding one's self

© Isaacs 2012

Public Speaking

This is a perfect type of job for some people with ASD. I have had a great experience of speaking on behalf of Autism Oxford which was such a positive experience. The preparation is excellent and it's about confidence in yourself, something I have being stating a lot, not without substance. Confidence brings out the best in people and for someone with an ASD who has a vast knowledge on a particular subject this would be a perfect opportunity for him or her to share their interests with people who will appreciate them. I can remember how nervous I felt before appearing on the stage in front of two hundred people, but as soon as I got on I was fine, I was in my element. I was talking about HFA and my experience; I was fine. Some people with ASDs are good talkers; we'd talk all day and night if we could!

Public Speaking Tips

> 1. *Find a place or organisation which revolves around your special interest.*
> 2. *Do lots of practice with writing and speaking, this will improve your literary and verbal skills.*

> 3. Seek out improvements (this can be very hard for someone with ASD but it will be beneficial in the long term).

Myself at an Autism Oxford Event 2011

Food For Thought

This can be an interesting subject and food can be a problem for people with ASDs. The concept of "sameness" can go to the extreme of having the same foods every day or avoiding certain foods for seemingly random reasons. When you feed the body you're also improving your brain functioning skills and one issue is having to be prompted at times to eat food. There have been times in my life where this has been a really serious issue and has bordered onto being anorexic. The point is what *IS* the issue? Is it sensory? Is it the taste? Or the look? Or the fact that when the *bean juice* goes onto the sausage it changes the food? Whatever the reason it must be found out so that meal times can be fun and enjoyable. It's a time to be together (which can be hard for people with ASDs).

Things to know

1. *Taste, texture, smell of the meal.*
2. *Does there have to be symmetry on the plate (foods not clashing with one another)?*

3. *Is it to do with body disconnectedness? (not understanding when the body is "telling" you it's hungry).*

4. *Is it decision making?*

5. *Once a reason has been found steps can be taken to help the individual with ASD cope and be happy at meal times.*

Food, Food, Food!

Personal Hygiene

This aspect is very important. If you have good hygiene people do judge you better and if you don't then people will comment. It can be either too much or too little. I can remember over brushing my teeth for years and years and although they're healthy the gums on my top back teeth have noticeably receded. When I was in my teens I had to be reminded to have a bath and wash. My Mother was bathing me until I was at an age in theory I should have been doing it myself. Again this is to do with prompting and understanding why someone needs to do this. People with ASDs do have an unusual hygiene procedure and I'm no exception. You need to find a balance because this can affect your health and make you more prominent to catching viruses and becoming ill more frequently. As people with ASDs rely on structure it could be a good idea to go through a structure with them.

Tips & Advice

1. *Have a mental list of things to do.*
2. *Have a list of things to do on a piece of paper with writing and/or pictures.*
3. *Make it an essential part of your routine, this will reduce the need for prompting.*

Things that you need for personal hygiene

© Isaacs 2012

Video Games

Video games are a big business. They're on the television, in magazines and they have improved over the years both through scope and technology. I still in my adult life like playing on computer games such as RPG adventure that has both depth and story.

However, when I was younger this obsession with video games was very unhealthy, causing temper tantrums and compulsive need for the game to be completed and replaying the same game over and over again. It's also caused headaches, dizziness, feelings of detachment and feelings of nausea. When you have HFA, as I have stated earlier, you are prone to obsessions and I think parents should certainly mediate their child's input on how much time they spend on computer games. It can cause a whole host of problems especially for children with HFA. I can remember getting very angry and this is no good. My parents took my console away and mediated with me how long I could play on the game. This was very good because they were creating structure and boundaries around this obsession.

Tips & Advice

1. Explain to the child with HFA what needs to be done and divert onto another subject.
2. Taking the game away isn't a bad thing; explain why and suggest other activities say for example drawing the characters from the game (use a positive alternative).
3. If the child with HFA seems a lot better in him/herself explain this to the child for positive self-reflection.

My Parents & How They Have Helped Me

My parents have helped me a lot over the years. That may sound like a cliché but its true and I'm glad they've always been there for me. They didn't have a label (a word which I dislike) for my behaviour. The words "*autism*" or "*autistic*" were not used they had to just get on with it. The sound discipline from my Mother (whom has Atypical Autism) has a lot to with this. When I was naughty I was told there was no two ways about it. Also my Mother *explained* what effect this would have on both her and my Father when I had a tantrum or had done something wrong. The act of self-reflection also helped with my mind blindness; it was forcing me to (at least) try and see how sometimes my actions have affected others.

My Father has grown to be very streetwise because of his background and upbringing. He has Asperger's Syndrome and has always given me advice on social situations because he can relate to my confusion and this has been very helpful in the workplace and in other social situations, such as when I meet up with friends or go to a pub etc. They have given me practical skills and advice which is essential for living. I thank them both for who they are and how much they have helped. It has inspired me to write this because with skills comes inspiration. A person with ASD is like a funnel with the water being social information, the funnel representing social input and the water in the bottle representing the slow progress one makes with HFA. Life is meant to be a positive journey no matter what anybody says or does. These practical steps I hope will help people with ASDs to achieve their goals. Because you have got to start somewhere haven't you?

Mum & Dad Christmas Holiday

© Isaacs 2012

Lightning Source UK Ltd.
Milton Keynes UK
UKOW040246050613